WATCH OUT!

page 2

page 14

Dee Reid

Story illustrated by
Tom Percival

 # Before Reading

In this story

 Rusty

 The old lady

Tricky words

- cross
- road
- don't
- want
- grabbed
- down

 Introduce these tricky words and help the reader when they come across them later!

Story starter

Rusty is a robot. He is old and rusty but he likes to help people. One day, Rusty saw an old lady by the zebra crossing. He thought she wanted to cross the road.

Rusty and the Crossing

"I can help you," said Rusty.

"I can help you to cross the road," said Rusty.

"I don't want you to help," said the old lady.

Rusty grabbed the old lady.

"Put me down!"
said the old lady.

"Put me down now!" said the old lady.

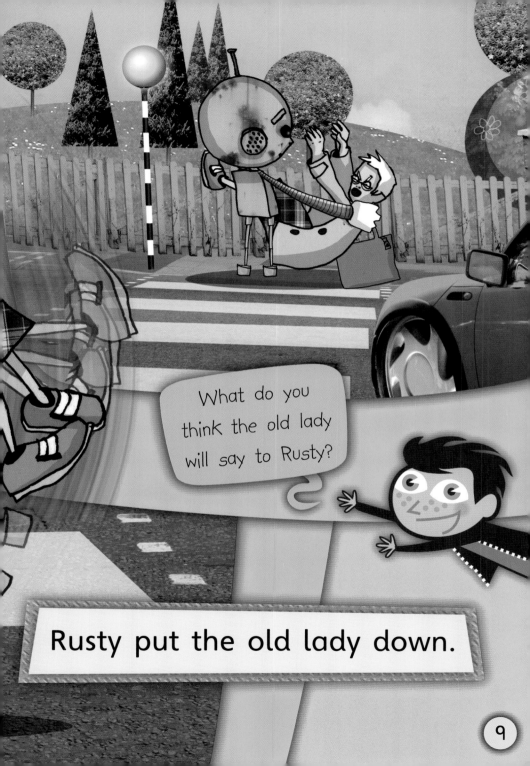

What do you think the old lady will say to Rusty?

Rusty put the old lady down.

"You rusty tin can," said the old lady. "Now I want to cross the road."

"I can help you," said Rusty.

Quiz

- Why was the old lady cross with Rusty?
- Do you think the old lady was still cross with Rusty at the end of the story?

Word Detective

- Phonic Focus: Initial phonemes

  Page 5: Find a word that starts with the phoneme 'w'.
- Page 5: Find a word that means 'do not'.
- Page 6: Find a word that rhymes with 'cold'.

Super Speller

Read this word:

me

Now try to spell it!

HA! HA! HA!

Q What did the traffic light say to the motorist?

A Don't look – I'm changing.

13

Find out about

- Where it is safe to cross the road

Tricky words

- safe
- cross
- near
- parked
- corner
- fast

Introduce these tricky words and help the reader when they come across them later!

Text starter

To keep safe you need to take care when crossing the road. Find a safe place to cross – not near a parked car or a corner. Best of all, cross at a zebra crossing or a pelican crossing.

Road Safety

Is it safe to cross here?

No, it is not safe.
It is too near a parked car.

Is it safe to cross here?

No, it is not safe.
It is too near a corner.

A car might come round the corner before you had time to cross.

Is it safe to cross here?

No, it is not safe.
The cars are going too fast.

Is it safe to cross here?

Yes, it is.
It is safe to cross here.

It is safe to cross here too!

Quiz

Text Detective

- Why is it safe to cross at a zebra crossing?
- How will you judge whether it is safe to cross a road?

Word Detective

- **Phonic Focus:** Initial phonemes
  Page 16: Find a word beginning with the phoneme 'c'.
- Page 16: Find a word that rhymes with 'got'.
- Page 16: Find the word 'is' twice on this page.

Super Speller

Read this word:

it

Now try to spell it!

HA! HA! HA!

Q What do you call a hedgehog that crosses a road?

A Lucky!